MAC, Information Detective,

in the case of ...

The Strangest Dinosaur That Never Was

Written by Dr. Marilyn P. Arnone

with Illustrations by Gerry Stockley

MAC, Information Detective,

in the case of ...

The Strangest Dinosaur That Never Was

ISBN Number 1-59158-147-8
Copyright © 2003
Libraries Unlimited
A Member of the Greenwood Publishing Group, Inc.
In Association with Creative Media Solutions, Oriental, NC

Cover Design by Anne Sabach

Guide for Educators and Parents

This book is designed as a read-aloud for students in primary grades as part of a school or at-home lesson or unit on evaluation skills. The three Interactive Pages provide opportunities for brainstorming and discussion as well as a *pausing place* to pick up the story at a later time to accommodate scheduling or varied attention spans.

Some children may not be familiar with the information literacy terms used in this book. Before reading *The Strangest Dinosaur That Never Was,* you may wish to discuss the terms **information, search, "narrow down," Internet, Web site, home page, author, links,** and **buttons.**

Acknowledgements

There are several people who deserve credit for helping get this project off the ground. They are Dr. Ruth V. Small for her expertise, guidance, and ever-present support; Tom Hardy for his advice and indispensable help in managing the project; Dr. Patricia Senn Breivik for her encouragement; Marie Sciretta for her careful review of the text and suggestions for increasing its comprehensibility for children in primary grades; Sharon Coatney and Edward Kurdyla for believing the book project had potential; Anne Sabach for adding her own creativity to the graphic design; Gerry Stockley for his artistic talent and dedication to this project; and my long-time friend and business partner, MariRae Dopke, for putting me in touch with the right artist for the project. Finally, I would like to acknowledge Syracuse University's Center for Digital Literacy for choosing this book to share with practitioners through one of its special projects.

About the Author

Dr. Marilyn Arnone has developed numerous media projects for the child audience in addition to co-authoring several books for educators including *Turning Kids On To Research: The Power of Motivation* with Dr. Ruth Small. Arnone is particularly interested in encouraging the kind of curiosity that drives learning and is currently developing a series of videos called *Young Researchers.* The videos follow students through the research process as they dig for answers to the questions they pose. She is Director of Educational Media at the Center for Digital Literacy and an adjunct professor at the School of Information Studies at Syracuse University, and is President of Research and Development at Creative Media Solutions, Oriental, NC.

Knock, Knock. "Hellooooo," called Sandy as she pounded on the door. The sign read "MAC I.D." I.D. stands for **Information Detective** and that's what MAC is. His office is located inside a big old tree.

MAC answered the door. "Hello, my name is MAC. What can I do for you?" he asked as he attempted to greet Sandy by shaking hands. "Ooops!" he said when the pile of paperwork he was carrying spilled to the floor. "Come on in."

"Hi. I'm Sandy. Since you are an expert on Web sites, I could really use your help," she said. "I am working on a very important school project. My topic is dinosaurs which sounds like a really big topic, I know. So, I narrowed it down. I decided to search for an unusual dinosaur, one that is very different than all the rest. While I was searching on the Internet for information, I found one that I had never even heard of!"

"Which dinosaur was that, Sandy?" asked MAC.

"It's called the Hammer-Nose Dinosaur. It roamed the earth about the same time as the ferocious Tyrannosaurus Rex. Lots of other kids are doing their projects on the T-Rex. Not me. I want to do mine on the Hammer-Nose Dinosaur because it's so strange and different!"

"Sounds great! So, why do you need me?" asked MAC, a little confused.

She asked MAC to type in the address of the Hammer-Nose Dinosaur Web site on his large screen computer. When he did, the home page (that's the starting place on a Web site) came up on screen. And there it was—the Hammer-Nose Dinosaur, the oddest-looking dinosaur ever! It had round features and a hammer-like nose that stuck way out. IIts eyelashes were long and quite curly. Right on top of its head, there was a crop of reddish hair that stuck out in all directions. Its stomach was spotted and very round. It had not two, not four, but *six* skinny arms, too! The Hammer-Nose Dinosaur didn't look at all ferocious, like the T-Rex.

"You are right about this dinosaur, Sandy. It sure is different," said MAC, not suspecting anything, yet. "So, what's the problem?" he added.

"Let me show you, MAC," she said as she clicked on the button that took her to a section of the Web site called *Hammer-Nose Facts*. Everything looked pretty official until Sandy pointed something out to MAC. "Look! It tells you about the Hammer-Nose Dinosaur's favorite snack! Its favorite snack is ROCKS!!! It eats small rocks every night before it goes to sleep. There's a picture of how it uses its nose to break up the larger rocks into pebble-sized rocks before it gulps them down."

What Do You Think?

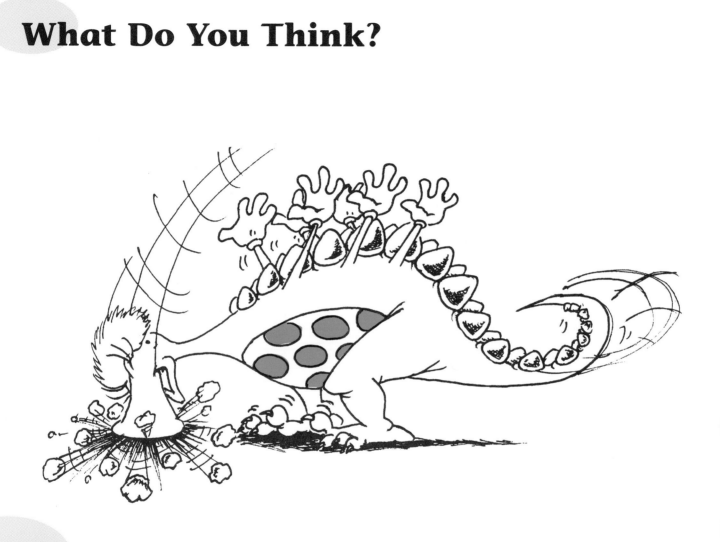

Does that seem a bit strange to you? Have you ever heard of a dinosaur that ate **rocks**? Do you know of *any* animal that eats rocks?

MAC didn't pick up
on the clue just yet.

"Hmmm," said MAC,
finally. "That is odd."

"Odd?" exclaimed Sandy in disbelief. "Of course it is odd, MAC! Have you ever heard of
any dinosaurs that ate **rocks**? Dinosaurs ate living things like plants and other animals.
Rocks are *NOT* living things!"

MAC was finally getting suspicious. "Hmmm. That could be a **clue** that something is not right here!" he declared with all the confidence of an **expert** in his field.

"Exactly!" said Sandy. "That's why I am confused. I was going to use this Web site for getting **information** for my project. Then, when I read that this dinosaur ate rocks, well, … it just didn't match up with what I know about dinosaurs and living things. What really confuses me is that this is on the **Internet**!"

"Soooooo?" asked MAC, curiously.

"So, I thought that if something was on the Internet, then it must be **true**!"

"No wonder you are confused," said MAC. "You see, Sandy, just because you find something on the Internet does **_not_** mean it's **true**!"

"That was what I was afraid of," said Sandy. "It just didn't add up. Now, what should I do? How will I know whether or not I can **believe** the information?"

Suddenly, MAC jumped up on his desk. He fluffed up his cape behind him and adjusted his detective cap. Then, he reached for his badge from under his cape and thrust it out, exclaiming, "This is a job for MAC, Information Detective!" With that, he jumped into the air like Superman. What do you think happened next?

"Ooops!" chuckled MAC after landing in a heap on the floor. His tumble didn't seem to bother him at all. He simply sprang to his feet and dusted himself off.

"Where was I?" he mumbled. "Oh yes, we need to look for **clues** that will let us know if you can **trust** the information you found!" said MAC. "Say, I could probably use your help on this assignment, Sandy. Would you like to become a *Junior Information Detective*?"

"Sure, MAC! Where do we start?" said Sandy eager to begin searching for clues.

"Not too fast," said MAC. "First, you will have to learn what clues to look for. Come on over to the *MAC School for Information Detectives* and I'll show you."

What Do You Think?

Can you think of any **clues** that might help you decide
if the **information** on a Web site is **true** or not?

Let's turn the page and see what's going on at the
MAC School for Information Detectives.

At the school, MAC and the children worked to make a chart of clues. This helped them find out if a Web site is a good one, a poor one, or one that needs lots of improvement.

THINGS TO LOOK FOR IN A WEBSITE:

GOOD	POOR	NEEDS IMPROVEMENT
INFORMATIVE	• NO WAY TO CHECK IF INFO IS TRUE	
GOOD LAYOUT	• BROKEN LINKS	
CATEGORIZED	• THINGS DON'T WORK THE WAY THEY SHOULD LIKE THE BUTTONS THAT DO NOTHING	
PLEASING TO THE EYE		

For example, a poor Web site is one there is no way to **check** whether the information is **true**. Or where things just do not work the way they should, like **buttons** that do nothing or **links** that are broken.

When MAC was convinced that Sandy was ready, he took out a brand new badge and pinned it on her shirt. She was now a *Junior Information Detective*! Sandy was very proud. Now, it was time to get to work.

The most important thing that Sandy and MAC need to investigate about the Hammer-Nose Dinosaur Web site is whether the **information** is **true** or *correct*.

Do you think there ever really was a Hammer-Nose Dinosaur?

Let's see what MAC and Sandy will do.

Back at his office, MAC unveils a wacky-looking contraption.

"This is one of my new inventions, Sandy. I call it the *Truth-O-Meter*. Let's plug in the **address** of the Hammer-Nose Dinosaur Web site and see if the Truth-O-Meter thinks the information is true or not."

"Is that all there is to it?" asked Sandy.

"Yep, if it works the way it's supposed to," said MAC concentrating on adjusting the knobs and buttons on the machine. "There. When I press this last button, we should have our answer."

MAC's silly invention made all sorts of weird noises. Then, it shook and rattled until finally, the Truth-O-Meter just petered out. "Putt, Putt, Poof!"

"I thought that was just too easy, MAC," said a disappointed Sandy.

"I guess we'll do things the good old fashioned way," said MAC, not at all upset that his invention didn't work. "I'll have to think of a new design, that's all. For now, let's go back to the computer."

"First, we will check to see if there is any information on the **author** of the Web site. That's the person who is responsible for the information there. O.K., right here on the home page it says the author is Eko Jasti. That's a different name. But who *is* he?"

MAC and Sandy looked everywhere to see if there was any information on Eko. No place did it tell whether Eko was an **expert** on dinosaurs or not. An *expert* is someone who knows a lot about a certain subject. There wasn't even a way to contact the author to ask questions. A good Web site should give you a way to get more information if you need it, like emailing the author, for example. MAC and Sandy would have to look for other clues to find out whether the information on this Web site was true or not.

What Do You Think?

Sandy and MAC have a problem. There is no way to contact the **author** of the Web site. Can you think of other ways they can **check** the **information** about the Hammer-Nose Dinosaur? Is there someone who could help? Who would *you* ask?

A s an experienced Information Detective, MAC came up with a good idea. He and Sandy visited the school library. They asked Mrs. Johnstone, the librarian, if she could help them find books on the Hammer-Nose Dinosaur. She searched and searched but could not find a single one.

"Hmmm," muttered MAC as he tapped his pencil on his clipboard that held a checklist of clues. "This isn't looking good so far. No information on the author." He crossed it off the list. "No way to contact the author." He crossed this off the list, too. "No information on the Hammer-Nose Dinosaur in books." Again, he crossed it off the list. "Ooops!" MAC had pressed so hard with his pencil on the paper that he broke the tip. They thanked Mrs. Johnstone for her help and went to search for other clues. Sandy was worried.

"Does that mean that the Hammer-Nose Dinosaur doesn't exist?" Sandy asked sadly as they were leaving the library. She had her heart set on **researching** this dinosaur for her project.

"We aren't finished digging for clues, yet, Sandy," said MAC confidently. "So, don't give up!"

"O.K., MAC," said Sandy, "but where do we look next?"

"I'm thinking. I'm thinking," said MAC trying hard to come up with an answer. Then Sandy had an idea …

"How about asking an **expert**? Someone who knows a lot about dinosaurs?"

"**B**rilliant idea! I was just about to suggest that," said MAC. "I trained you well, Sandy. You are becoming an excellent Junior Information Detective. Let's head back to the office and make some calls."

So off they went.

When they arrived back at MAC's office, MAC and Sandy logged onto the Internet and found a Web site on dinosaurs that was sponsored by an organization with a good reputation. In fact, Sandy's science teacher had shown them the Web site a few weeks earlier. The Web site included several experts on dinosaurs who helped to author the site.

"O.K., Sandy," said MAC. "Look there." He pointed at the address and phone number given for each of the dinosaur experts. Then, he picked up the telephone and dialed the number of Professor Young, one of the experts listed. He handed the phone to Sandy. "You can take it from here," he said.

"I'm a little nervous," she said. "What if Professor Young thinks my question is stupid?"

"No question is stupid," said MAC. "Just relax. He will admire that you take your project seriously enough to ask an expert for help."

oon, Professor Young answered the phone. "Hello. This is Professor Young." Sandy told the Professor all about the Hammer-Nose Dinosaur and the Web site. After listening very carefully, the professor told her what she already suspected.

"I am sorry to have to tell you this, Sandy. But there is no Hammer-Nose Dinosaur. I have been doing **research** for years and have never heard of such a creature."

"Oh, no!" said a disappointed Sandy. "You mean there never was a Hammer-Nose Dinosaur?"

"I'm afraid not," said the Professor. He could tell that Sandy was upset. "But, I do know of another unusual dinosaur that really did exist. Maybe you would like to do your project on it!"

Sandy was so excited. MAC handed her a pencil and paper and Sandy took **notes** on everything the professor told her about the unusual dinosaur that really did exist thousands of years ago. He even gave her ideas on where she could find more information, like books, Web sites, and even science magazines. Sandy wasn't sad now. She didn't care anymore about the Hammer-Nose Dinosaur. She knew she had found a terrific **topic** for her project.

The professor was still curious about the Hammer-Nose Dinosaur Web site. "Who was the author of the Web site?" he asked. Sandy told him it was Eko Jasti. The professor laughed.

"What's so funny?" asked Sandy.

The professor told Sandy to write the name backwards. She did. Then she moved the letters around a little. After spacing out the letters, it read, "It's a joke." MAC and Sandy were so surprised. It had been someone's idea of a joke all along. What a terrible joke! She thanked the professor for his help and said goodbye. **Sandy had learned a valuable lesson.**

She turned to MAC and said, "Now, I understand, MAC. You just can't believe everything you find on the Internet. You need to **check** to see if the **information** is **true**."

"**Y**ou're right, Sandy! Sometimes, the information you find may not have the right facts. Or the information may be **out-of-date** and too old to be helpful to you. Some information, like you discovered, may just be a joke, or what we call in the information investigation business, a **hoax**. So, always **check** your information. You have done a super job of helping me solve this case, Sandy. But remember, there is also *good* information on the Internet. If you need help finding information you can trust, ask your school librarian or teacher."

Now that the case was solved, it was time for MAC to give it a name. He always likes doing that.

"This case is closed," roared a proud MAC hopping on top of his desk. "I think I will call it the case of ...

The Strangest Dinosaur That Never Was!"

With that, MAC fluffed up his cape, posing like Superman and standing as tall as he possibly could. With his arms stretched way in front of him, he leaped into the air and ...

Well ...

what do *YOU* think happened?

Turn the page and find out ...

Yes, MAC landed in a big heap on the floor! Sandy gently helped him up and dusted him off.

"I'll get it next time!" he said, with a twinkle in his eye.

THE END